A to Z of Dinosaurs and Prehistoric Animals

Quarto is the authority on a wide range of topics.

Quarto educates, entertains and enriches the lives of our readers—enthusiasts and lovers of hands-on living.

www.quartoknows.com

Written by Nancy Dickmann

Design and editorial: Evolution Design & Digital Ltd (Kent)

This edition first published in 2020 by QED Publishing,
an imprint of The Quarto Group.
The Old Brewery, 6 Blundell Street,
London N7 9BH, United Kingdom.
T (0)20 7700 6700 F (0)20 7700 8066
www.QuartoKnows.com

A catalogue record for this book is available from the British Library.

ISBN 978-0-7112-5688-0

Manufactured in Guangdong, China CC042020

9 8 7 6 5 4 3 2 1

MIX
Paper from
responsible sources
FSC® C008047

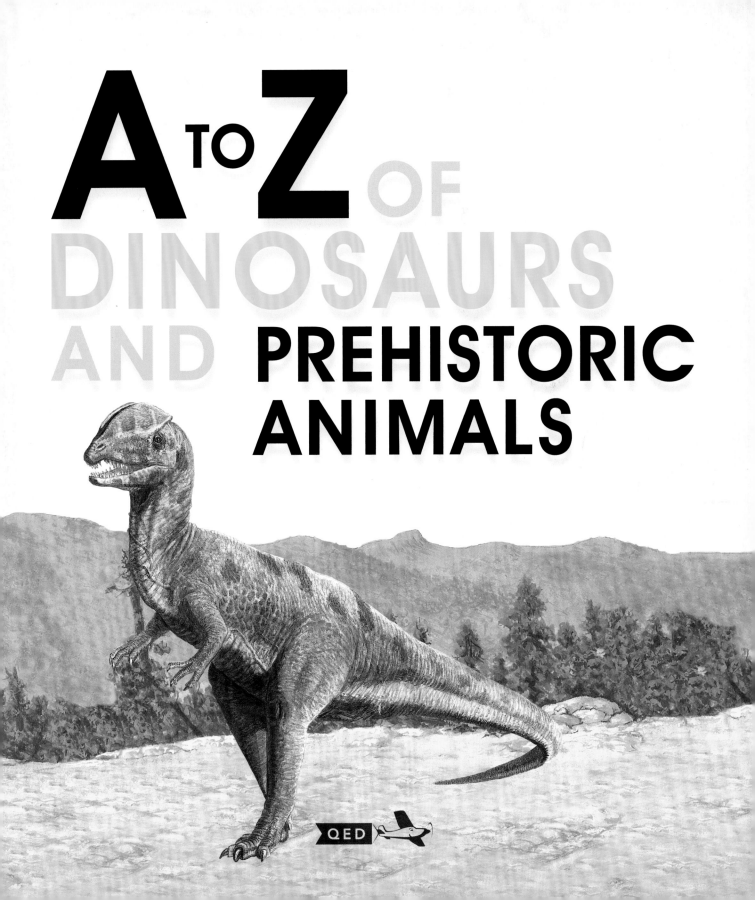

A TO Z OF DINOSAURS AND PREHISTORIC ANIMALS

QED

CONTENTS

WHAT IS A DINOSAUR?

Millions of years ago, dinosaurs roamed the Earth. Some were big and others were small; some were fierce hunters while others were peaceful plant-eaters. Although there were more than one thousand different **species** in every shape and size, all dinosaurs did have a few things in common.

Reptile Relatives

Dinosaurs are all part of a group of animals called **reptiles**. Reptiles such as lizards, crocodiles, snakes and tortoises are still alive today. Like those animals, dinosaurs hatched from eggs. But while many dinosaurs were covered with scaly skin like today's reptiles, some dinosaurs had bodies covered with feathers instead.

Hips Don't Lie

Dinosaurs can be divided into two groups based on the shape of their hips. Bird-hipped dinosaurs were plant-eaters, such as *Iguanodon*. Their pubis bone pointed downwards and towards the tail, like that of modern birds. Lizard-hipped dinosaurs included fierce, meat-eating creatures like *Tyrannosaurus rex*, and also plant-eaters such as *Diplodocus*. Their pubis bone pointed downwards and towards the front, like that of a lizard.

WHAT DID DINOSAURS LOOK LIKE?

Dinosaurs all lived on land, so they had legs for walking rather than flippers or wings. All dinosaurs had four limbs. In some species, the limbs were roughly the same size, allowing the dinosaur to walk on four legs. In other species, the front limbs were much smaller, more like arms, and the dinosaur walked or ran on their hind legs.

Special Skulls

The skull of a dinosaur has some interesting features. All dinosaurs had two holes behind the eye socket. Their jaw muscles went through these holes and attached directly to the top of the skull. This gave dinosaurs a very powerful bite. Every dinosaur also had an extra hole in their skull, between the eye socket and the nostril, which affected how the dinosaur breathed.

Spots or Stripes?

Pictures of dinosaurs often show them with grey, brown or dark green skin. But this is just a guess! It is incredibly rare to find fossilized dinosaur skin, and **palaeontologists** can't tell its original colour. Dinosaurs may have been brightly coloured, or possibly even patterned with spots or stripes.

PREHISTORIC ANIMALS

Dinosaurs weren't the only creatures living in prehistoric times. There were also other types of animals, such as early **mammals**, sharing the land. There were fish and other species of reptiles swimming in the sea, and winged reptiles swooping through the air.

Mammals

The earliest mammals were tiny, mouselike creatures that first appeared about 200 million years ago, not long after the first dinosaurs. They laid eggs, like a few species of mammals do today. Early mammals were mainly small, but after the dinosaurs died out, they began to get much bigger. Some of them swam in the sea, like today's dolphins and whales.

Flying and Swimming

All dinosaurs lived on land, but other types of prehistoric reptiles – called **pterosaurs** – were able to fly. Their name means 'winged lizard', but these animals were covered with feathers and were more closely related to birds than to today's lizards. At the same time, swimming reptiles such as plesiosaurs hunted in the oceans.

THE PREHISTORIC WORLD

Dinosaurs roamed a planet that looked very different from the Earth today. All of the **continents** were squashed together to form one giant supercontinent called Pangea. In the period before the dinosaurs there had been a large variety of fish and other creatures living on land and in the ocean. But most of them became **extinct** about 250 million years ago, clearing the way for the dinosaurs.

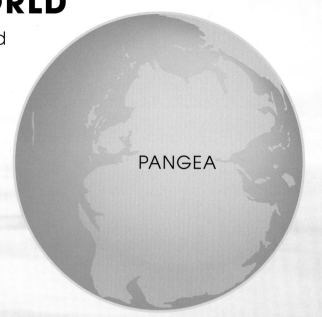

PANGEA

Weather and Climate

There was no ice at the poles during this period, and the temperature differences from one part of the world to another were small. Because much of the land was so far from the sea, **geologists** think that it was likely to be fairly dry, though there may have been rainy seasons similar to today's monsoons. As the continents began to break apart, the **climate** became more humid.

Plant Life

The land during this period was covered with ferns and plants called cycads, which look a bit like palm trees. Taller trees were conifers, the **ancestors** of today's pine and spruce trees. There were no flowers at the beginning of the age of the dinosaurs – they first appeared about 140 million years ago.

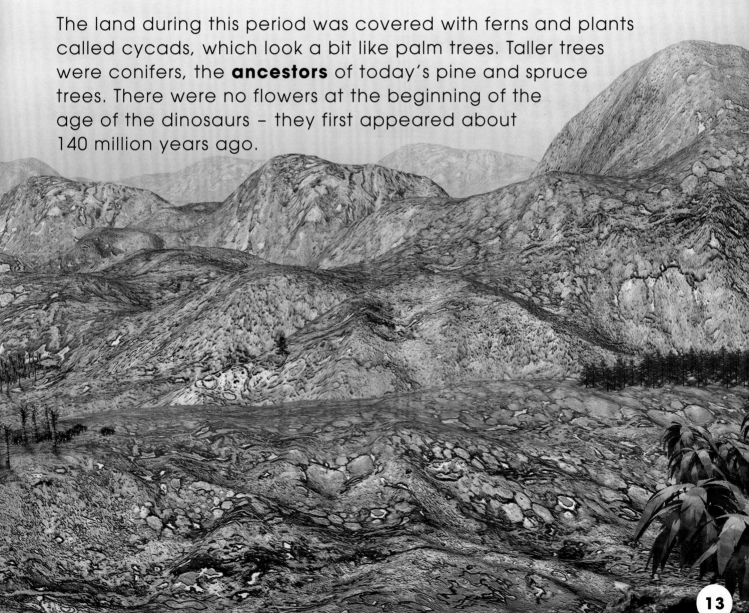

A

Allosaurus

Lived: Late Jurassic

Size: Up to 12.2 metres long

Diet: Meat

Allosaurus belonged to the group of dinosaurs known as **theropods** – fierce **carnivores** that could walk and run on their hind legs. An *Allosaurus's* front limbs were small, but they had three sharp claws for grasping **prey**. *Allosaurus* had thick ridges over its eyes. Its thick tail helped it to balance as it ran after its prey.

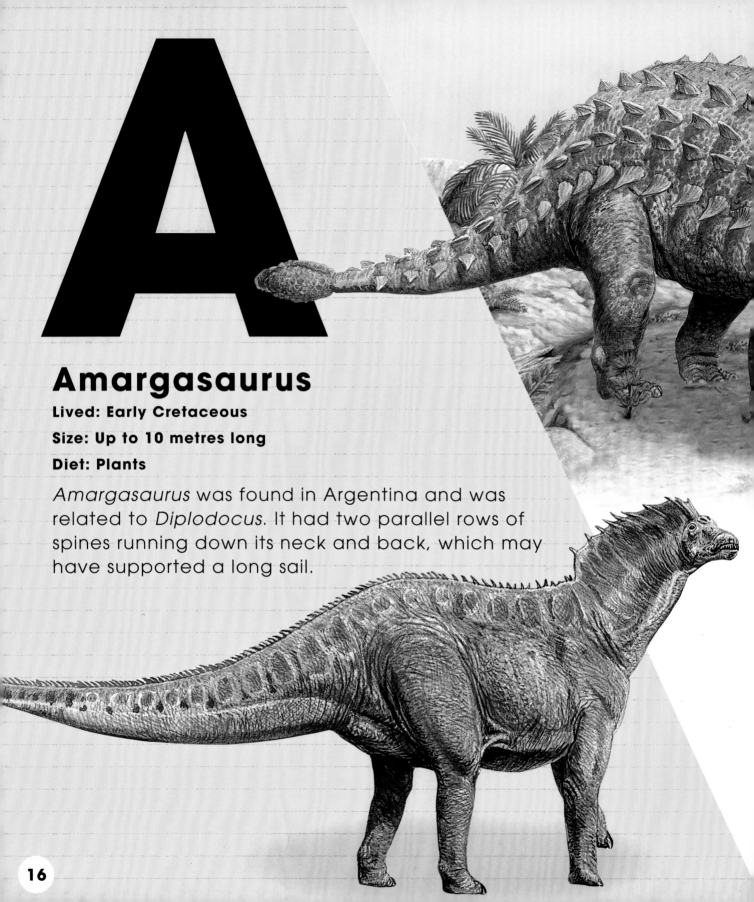

A

Amargasaurus

Lived: Early Cretaceous

Size: Up to 10 metres long

Diet: Plants

Amargasaurus was found in Argentina and was related to *Diplodocus*. It had two parallel rows of spines running down its neck and back, which may have supported a long sail.

Archaeopteryx

Lived: Late Jurassic

Size: 46 centimetres long

Diet: Meat

Fossils show that *Archaeopteryx* had feathers on its wings, allowing it to fly or glide through the air. This small dinosaur may have used its long tail for balance as it attacked prey with sharp teeth and clawed fingers.

Ankylosaurus

Lived: Late Cretaceous

Size: Up to 7 metres long

Diet: Plants

Ankylosaurus was like a walking tank. It was heavy and slow, but the thick bony plates on its back helped to protect it from **predators**. The plates were covered with rows of bony spikes and knobs for extra protection. *Ankylosaurus* could swing its heavy clubbed tail to fight back against attackers.

A

ARMOUR

Prehistoric animals had to face some of history's most terrifying predators, such as *Tyrannosaurus rex* and *Giganotosaurus*. Some smaller animals relied on speed or hiding to escape, but others **evolved** bodies that could help to protect them.

Thick Skin

Dinosaurs such as *Ankylosaurus* and *Euoplocephalus* were slow-moving **herbivores** with bony plates that completely covered their back and sides. The plates were often covered with hard studs or horns. Some mammals and reptiles had armour or shells too. Some animals also had a club or spike at the end of their tail that they could use to swing at predators.

Spikes and Spines

Other dinosaurs used spikes and spines for protection – and maybe even for fighting back. Some, such as *Stegosaurus*, had spikes at the end of their tail. One of *Stegosaurus's* relatives, *Gigantspinosaurus*, had a giant curved spike behind each shoulder. *Triceratops* had three sharp horns on its face that were used for fighting. *Styracosaurus* had large spikes on its neck **frill** as well as a horn on its face.

B

Bagaceratops

Lived: Late Cretaceous

Size: Up to 1 metre long

Diet: Plants

This small relative of the *Triceratops* has a name that means 'small horned face'. It used its sharp beak to bite leaves and needles off plants, then chewed them up with flat teeth that were adapted for grinding.

Barapasaurus

Lived: Early Jurassic

Size: Up to 14 metres long

Diet: Plants

Palaeontologists discovered *Barapasaurus* in India, and its name is a mixture of Greek and Bengali words that mean 'big-legged lizard'. This large, heavy dinosaur walked on four legs and used its long neck to reach up to tear leaves off branches.

B

Brachiosaurus

Lived: Late Jurassic

Size: Up to 30 metres long

Diet: Plants

Brachiosaurus was one of the heaviest and tallest dinosaurs that ever lived. Its remains have been found across Europe, Africa and North America. Its front legs were taller than its back legs, allowing it to reach its long neck even higher into trees. Palaeontologists once thought that these heavy animals might have spent a lot of their time in water, but now they believe that *Brachiosaurus* lived entirely on land.

C

Carcharodontosaurus

Lived: Late Cretaceous

Size: Up to 13.7 metres long

Diet: Meat

Carcharodontosaurus was a large theropod that was nearly as big as *Tyrannosaurus rex*, and just as fearsome. Its enormous jaws had sharp, sharklike teeth that explain how it got its name from *Carcharodon*, the scientific name for the great white shark.

Centrosaurus

Lived: Late Cretaceous

Size: Up to 6 metres long

Diet: Plants

This heavy plant-eater was a relative of *Triceratops*, but instead of having three horns on its face, it had only one. Its neck frill was smaller than that of its more famous cousin, but it had two curving 'hornlets' over its eyes.

Coelodonta Antiquitatis

Lived: Pleistocene

Size: Up to 3.8 metres long

Diet: Plants

This large creature was basically a woolly and slightly larger version of the rhinoceroses that live in Africa today. Early humans hunted this large mammal, and pictures of it appear in many prehistoric cave paintings.

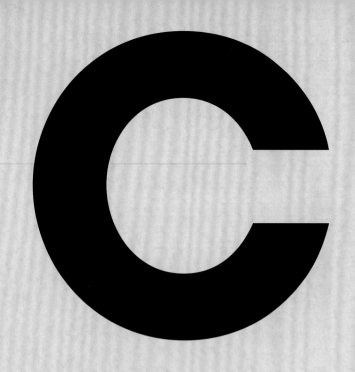

Coelophysis

Lived: Late Triassic

Size: Up to 2 metres long

Diet: Meat

Coelophysis lived at a time when dinosaurs were not yet at the top of the food chain. These small hunters had to compete for food with large reptiles. *Coelophysis* were small and agile, and their sharp teeth and claws gave them an advantage as they hunted small reptiles and insects.

Corythosaurus

Lived: Late Cretaceous

Size: Up to 10 metres long

Diet: Plants

Corythosaurus was part of a much larger group of medium-sized herbivores that walked on two legs. It gets its name from the hollow, helmet-shaped **crest** on its head. Its beak had no teeth, but rows of flat teeth on its jaws helped it to grind up leaves.

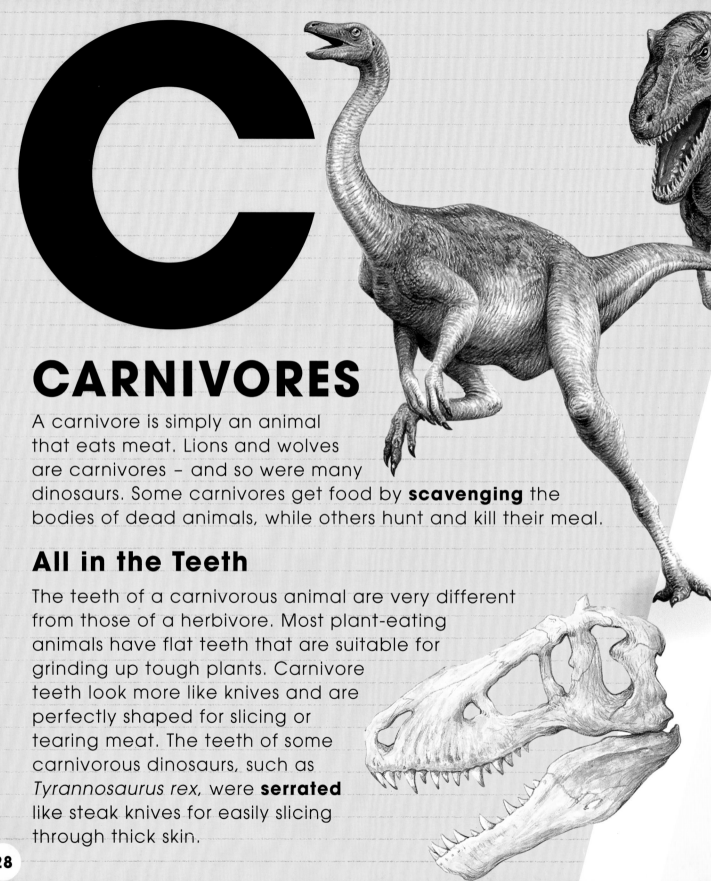

C

CARNIVORES

A carnivore is simply an animal that eats meat. Lions and wolves are carnivores – and so were many dinosaurs. Some carnivores get food by **scavenging** the bodies of dead animals, while others hunt and kill their meal.

All in the Teeth

The teeth of a carnivorous animal are very different from those of a herbivore. Most plant-eating animals have flat teeth that are suitable for grinding up tough plants. Carnivore teeth look more like knives and are perfectly shaped for slicing or tearing meat. The teeth of some carnivorous dinosaurs, such as *Tyrannosaurus rex*, were **serrated** like steak knives for easily slicing through thick skin.

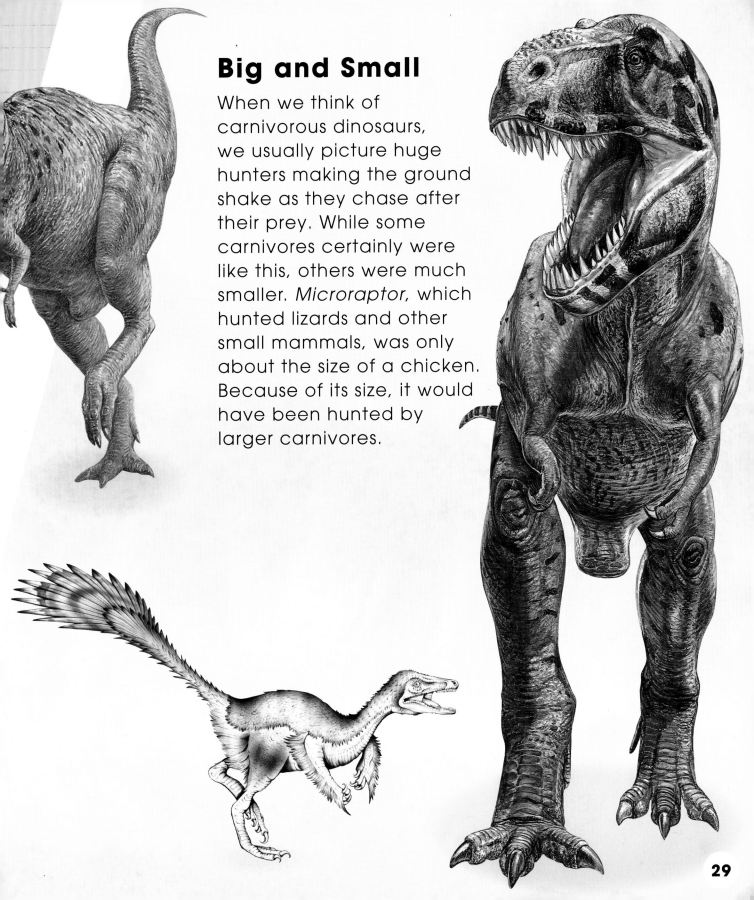

Big and Small

When we think of carnivorous dinosaurs, we usually picture huge hunters making the ground shake as they chase after their prey. While some carnivores certainly were like this, others were much smaller. *Microraptor*, which hunted lizards and other small mammals, was only about the size of a chicken. Because of its size, it would have been hunted by larger carnivores.

D

Dilophosaurus

Lived: Early Jurassic

Size: Up to 6 metres long

Diet: Meat

Although it was smaller than *Tyrannosaurus rex* and *Allosaurus, Dilophosaurus* was still a fast-moving predator. It had a pair of thin bony crests on its head, which may have been used to attract a mate or to send signals to other dinosaurs.

Diplodocus

Lived: Late Jurassic

Size: Up to 26 metres long

Diet: Plants

Diplodocus was a **sauropod** – a group of very large herbivores with long necks and tails that lumbered along on four strong legs. It once roamed the land that is now the western part of the United States. Fossilized or replica *Diplodocus* skeletons are displayed in museums around the world.

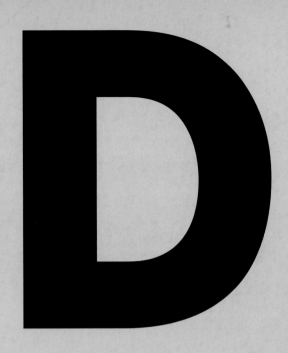

D

Doedicurus

Lived: Pleistocene

Size: Up to 4 metres long

Diet: Plants

This huge early mammal was an ancestor of today's armadillos. It had a huge dome-shaped shell made up of tightly fitting plates called scutes, which helped to protect it from predators. *Doedicurus* also had sharp spikes on its clubbed tail, which may have been a second line of defence.

Dryosaurus

Lived: Late Jurassic

Size: Up to 4.3 metres long

Diet: Plants

Dryosaurus was a relatively small dinosaur that walked on two legs. It used the fingers on its short front limbs to help grasp food as it grazed. It would have had to escape large predators such as *Allosaurus* if it wanted to survive.

E

Edaphosaurus

Lived: Late Carboniferous to Early Permian

Size: Up to 3.5 metres long

Diet: Plants

Edaphosaurus looks a bit like a dinosaur, but it lived before the dinosaurs, and it was more closely related to mammals than it was to reptiles or birds. It had a small head, short legs and an impressive sail-like fin along its back.

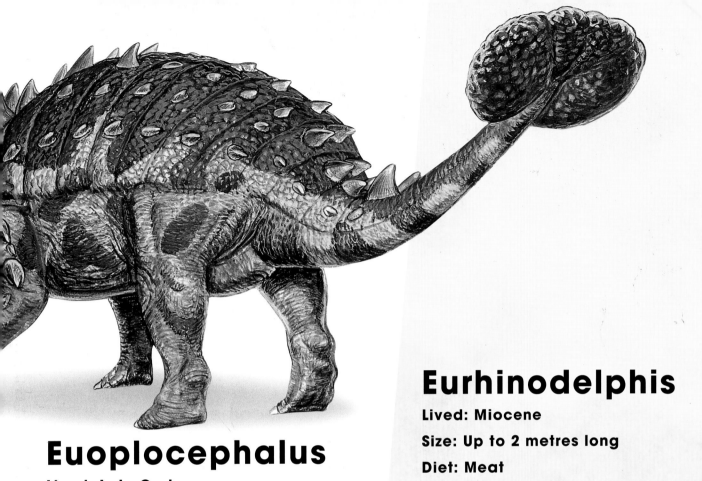

Euoplocephalus

Lived: Late Cretaceous

Size: Up to 7 metres long

Diet: Plants

Euoplocephalus was a close relative of *Ankylosaurus* and it had the same type of armoured body, though it was not quite as heavy. *Euoplocephalus* skeletons have never been found close together, so palaeontologists think these grazers lived a solitary life.

Eurhinodelphis

Lived: Miocene

Size: Up to 2 metres long

Diet: Meat

This ocean mammal was an ancestor of today's dolphins and porpoises, but it had a sharp snout that is more like that of a modern swordfish. It may have used its snout to hit or stab prey before grabbing them with its sharp teeth.

EXTINCTION

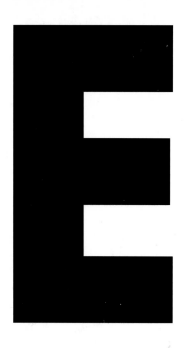

Dinosaurs walked the Earth for about 180 million years. During that time, new species evolved and others died out. For example, *Triceratops* never had to worry about being hunted by *Allosaurus* – that predator had already died out by the time *Triceratops* first appeared. When a species dies out entirely, it is said to be extinct.

The End of the Dinosaurs

Nearly all the remaining dinosaur species became extinct about 66 million years ago. No one is completely sure why this happened. Geologists have found evidence that a massive **asteroid** crashed into the Earth around this time. It would have destroyed many **habitats** and changed the climate, making it harder for dinosaurs to survive. Changes to the climate might also have been caused by volcanic eruptions.

Survivors

Whatever the cause, about 80 per cent of all animal species became extinct. But that means that 20 per cent survived. Among these were many mammals and non-dinosaur reptiles such as lizards and snakes. The only dinosaurs to survive were those that evolved into today's birds.

F

Falcarius

Lived: Early Cretaceous

Size: Up to 4 metres long

Diet: Plants

Falcarius means 'sickle cutter' – they had sharp, curved claws in the shape of a sickle. Palaeontologists think that they may have been covered with downy feathers.

Falcatus

Lived: Early Carboniferous

Size: About 30 centimetres long

Diet: Meat

This was a sharklike creature that lived in the ocean. Male *Falcatus* had a swordlike spine that was almost certainly used for attracting a mate. They had very big eyes that were probably for hunting in deep water where there is less light.

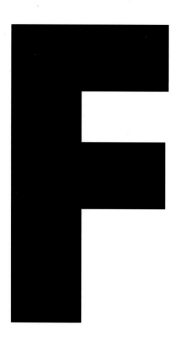

F

FLYING REPTILES

Although dinosaurs couldn't fly, they were related to reptiles that could. These pterosaurs were the first **vertebrates** ever to take to the skies. Many of them swooped down as they flew over oceans or lakes, scooping up fish to eat.

Skin Wings

The bodies of many pterosaurs were covered with primitive feathers that were small and tufty. However, their wings were made of skin, like the wings of a bat. Each front limb on a pterosaur had three clawed fingers, and a much longer fourth finger that supported the wing.

Here Today, Gone Tomorrow

Different species of pterosaurs lived throughout the time periods when dinosaurs roamed. When most of the remaining dinosaurs disappeared about 66 million years ago, so did the pterosaurs. They are not the ancestors of the birds or bats that fly today.

FOSSILS

The remains of ancient plants or animals left behind in rock are called fossils. Sometimes just the impression of the living thing is left behind. At other times, hard parts, such as bones and teeth, are turned to stone. Insects are often preserved when they are trapped in sticky sap, which hardens into amber.

The Lucky Few

It takes many thousands of years for a dead body to turn into a fossil, and the conditions have to be just right for it to happen at all. If sand or mud buries a body before it has time to rot away completely, it has a good chance of becoming a fossil.

How It Happens

Once the remains of a plant or animal are covered with sand or mud, the body stops rotting. As more layers of sand or mud pile up, the weight presses down on the lower layers. Eventually the layers turn into rock. Inside the rock, the minerals left behind by water merge with the remains to create a rocky copy of the plant or animal.

Other Fossils

Not all fossils are body parts! Palaeontologists have found many coprolites, which are fossilized poo. They also study fossilized nests, **burrows** and footprints.

Gerrothorax

Lived: Triassic

Size: About 1 metre long

Diet: Meat

This unusual-looking creature was an **amphibian** that lived mainly in water. Its eyes pointed upwards, which would have helped it to look for prey as it lay in wait on the bed of a river or lake.

Giganotosaurus

Lived: Early Cretaceous

Size: Up to 13 metres long

Diet: Meat

This fierce predator was taller and longer than a *Tyrannosaurus rex*, but not as heavy. It hunted the young of huge plant-eaters such as *Argentinosaurus*. Despite its size, it was a fast mover, and it could snap shut its huge jaws quickly to bring down prey.

Glossotherium

Lived: Late Pliocene to Early Holocene

Size: 4 metres long

Diet: Plants

Glossotherium was a type of prehistoric sloth, although it was much larger than the sloths that live today, and it lived on the ground rather than in trees. Early humans hunted these slow-moving sloths with stone-tipped spears.

G

GEOLOGICAL PERIODS

The history of the Earth covers so many billions of years that geologists break it up into chunks to make it easier to understand. The boundaries between the different time periods are based on differences in the rocks and the life forms that existed at the time.

Dinosaurs

Earth's history is divided into four eons. Eons are divided into eras, eras are divided into periods, periods into epochs. Dinosaurs lived in an era called the Mesozoic, which lasted from about 251 to 66 million years ago. It is divided into three periods: Triassic, Jurassic and Cretaceous.

Where Are We Now?

We are now in the Quaternary period, part of the Cenozoic era in the Phanerozoic eon. The epoch, which began about 12,000 years ago, is currently called the Holocene. But many scientists want to rename the period since 1950 as the Anthropocene. The new name shows that this is a time when human activities are changing the Earth's oceans, **atmosphere** and landscapes.

EON	ERA	PERIOD		EPOCH
Hadean				
Archean				
Proterozoic				
Phanerozoic	Palaeozoic	Cambrian		
		Ordovician		
		Silurian		
		Devonian		
		Carboniferous	Mississippian	
			Pennsylvanian	
		Permian		
	Mesozoic	**Triassic**		
		Jurassic		
		Cretaceous		
	Cenozoic	Palaeogene		Palaeocene
				Eocene
				Oligocene
		Neogene		Miocene
				Pliocene
		Quaternary		Pleistocene
				Holocene

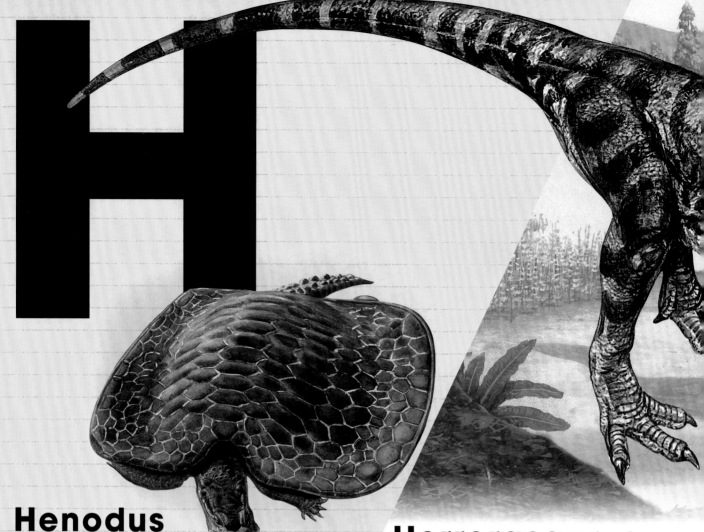

H

Henodus

Lived: Late Triassic

Size: About 1 metre long

Diet: Plants

Henodus was a type of early marine reptile that looks like a turtle with a flat, extra-wide shell. The shell would have provided protection from predators as *Henodus* fed on water plants.

Herrerasaurus

Lived: Late Triassic

Size: Up to 3 metres long

Diet: Meat

Herrerasaurus is one of the earliest known dinosaurs. It looked like a smaller version of later theropods such as *Allosaurus*, but their skeletons have some important differences. *Herrerasaurus* had a double-hinged jaw that let it tear off large chunks of meat.

Hypacrosaurus

Lived: Late Cretaceous

Size: Up to 9 metres long

Diet: Plants

Hypacrosaurus was part of the hadrosaur family of **duck-billed** dinosaurs. The high ridge running along its backbone may have helped it to regulate its body temperature. Palaeontologists have found fossilized nests, eggs and hatchlings from this species.

H

HERBIVORES

Herbivores get all the energy they need from eating plants. During the time of the dinosaurs, there were many more herbivores than there were carnivores. Herbivores roamed the land, grazing on grasses and leaves.

Herbivore Teeth

The teeth of plant-eating dinosaurs came in different forms. Many herbivores had flat, slablike teeth for grinding plants. Some herbivores, such as the long-necked *Brachiosaurus*, couldn't chew at all. They had peglike teeth for raking leaves from trees, which they then swallowed whole. Other herbivores had sharp beaks for ripping off leaves and twigs.

Big and Beautiful

Some herbivores were small. Others, such as *Stegosaurus*, were medium-sized. But the herbivores belonging to the group called sauropods were truly enormous! This group included *Diplodocus*, which was longer than a tennis court, and *Barapasaurus*. They walked on four strong legs and used their long necks to reach food.

Safety in Numbers

Palaeontologists have discovered that some types of herbivores lived and travelled in large **herds**. This may have helped them to keep safe from predators.

Ichthyosaurus

Lived: Late Triassic to Early Jurassic

Size: 3 metres long

Diet: Meat

Ichthyosaurus means 'fish lizard', and this ocean-dwelling reptile looked like a cross between a fish and a dolphin. They had pointed heads, conical teeth and flippers instead of arms and legs.

Indricotherium

Lived: Late Oligocene to Early Miocene

Size: 8 metres long

Diet: Plants

This ancestor of the rhinoceros had no horn, but it was the largest land mammal that ever lived, weighing four times as much as a modern elephant. Its long neck and front legs allowed it to reach up into trees to eat leaves.

Iguanodon

Lived: Early Cretaceous

Size: Up to 9 metres long

Diet: Plants

Iguanodon was one of the first dinosaurs to be discovered and studied. It could walk on two legs or four, and its thumb evolved into a spike that might have served as a weapon. After finding the fossilized remains of *Iguanodon*, palaeontologists first thought the spike belonged on its nose!

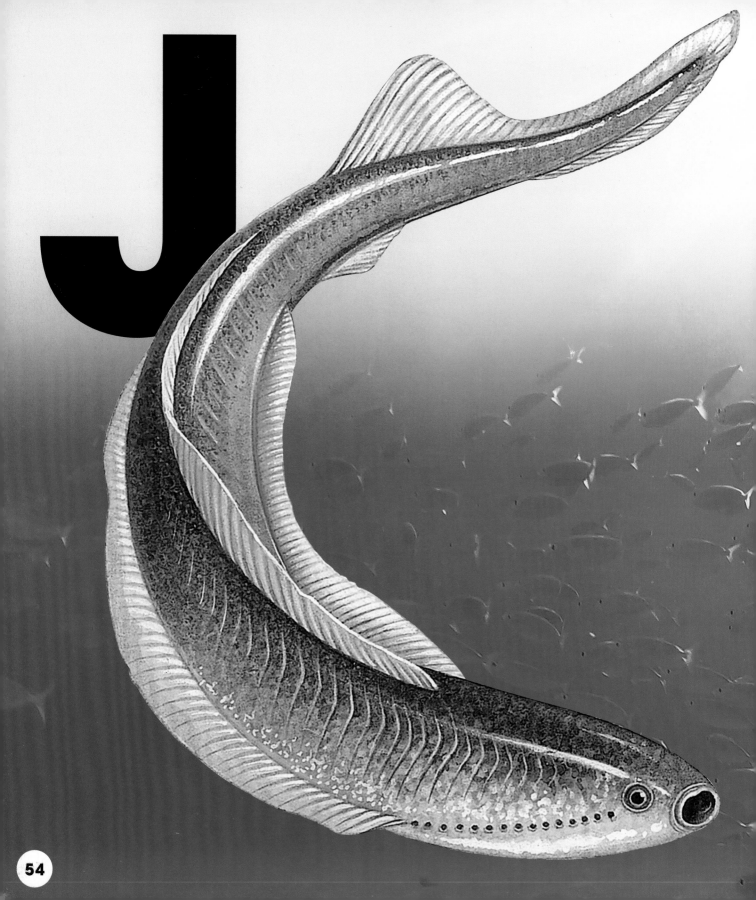

J

Jamoytius

Lived: Silurian

Size: About 25 centimetres long

Diet: Meat

Jamoytius lived about 200 million years before the first dinosaurs appeared. It was a small, jawless fish with a skeleton made of **cartilage**. Palaeontologists aren't sure how it fed; it may have latched on to other fish and sucked their blood like today's lampreys, which it resembles, or it may have sucked smaller fish into its mouth.

K

Karaurus

Lived: Late Jurassic

Size: About 20 centimetres long

Diet: Meat

Karaurus was very similar to its relative, the modern-day salamander. It probably hunted snails, worms, shellfish and insects in the waters of the late Jurassic.

Kritosaurus

Lived: Late Cretaceous

Size: About 8 metres long

Diet: Plants

Kritosaurus was a duck-billed dinosaur with a ridge of bone just below its eyes. It was first discovered in 1904 by Barnum Brown, who had discovered *Tyrannosaurus rex* just two years earlier. The plant-eating *Kritosaurus* had flat teeth that were continually being replaced as they wore down.

Lambeosaurus

Lived: Late Cretaceous

Size: About 9 metres long

Diet: Plants

Lambeosaurus stands out from other hadrosaurs thanks to its large size and the unusually shaped hollow crest on its head. Palaeontologists have found fossilized skin from this dinosaur that shows it had a pebbly texture.

Leptoceratops

Lived: Late Cretaceous

Size: About 3 metres long

Diet: Plants

Leptoceratops first appeared not long before the dinosaurs died out. Although it was related to *Triceratops*, it had no horns on its head, but it did have a small neck frill. It could probably walk on either two legs or four.

Lexovisaurus

Lived: Middle Jurassic

Size: 4.9 metres long

Diet: Plants

Fossilized remains of *Lexovisaurus* have been found in England and France. This slow-moving plant-eater was closely related to *Stegosaurus*. For defence against predators, it had thick skin and pointed spikes.

Longisquama

Lived: Middle or Late Triassic

Size: Unknown, but probably less than 30 centimetres long

Diet: Insects

Longisquama has been puzzling palaeontologists since it was first discovered. A complete skeleton hasn't yet been found, but it seems to have looked like a small lizard. However, it had long body parts that might have been scales or even feathers. It's also possible they could have belonged to a nearby plant rather than being attached to the animal!

Lystrosaurus

Lived: Late Permian to Early Triassic

Size: Up to 2.4 metres long

Diet: Plants

Lystrosaurus had no teeth, but it did have a horned beak for tearing off plant parts, and two tusks that it could use to dig up plant roots. Huge numbers of these creatures roamed the land in the early Triassic, in the period after a mass extinction killed off many of the large carnivores that might have hunted it.

M

Maiasaura

Lived: Late Cretaceous

Size: Up to 9 metres long

Diet: Plants

A fossilized *Maiasaura* nesting site discovered in 1978 provided evidence that at least some species of dinosaurs cared for their young. Adults of this duck-billed species were found alongside younger dinosaurs, hatchlings and broken eggshells.

Mammuthus primigenius

Lived: Middle Pleistocene to Early Holocene

Size: Up to 4 metres tall

Diet: Plants

Better known as woolly mammoths, these huge creatures were closely related to elephants. We know a lot about them, thanks to the large numbers of frozen bodies that have been found, complete with skin and fur. They also appear in cave paintings made by early human hunters, who ate their meat and used their bones to build homes.

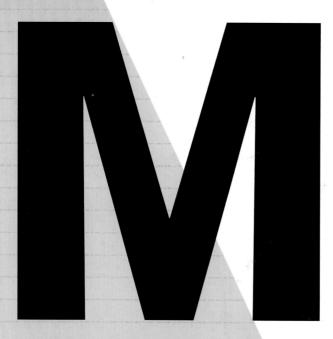

Massospondylus

Lived: Early Jurassic

Size: 4 metres long

Diet: Plants

Massospondylus was part of a group that formed the ancestors of the sauropods. It was the same basic shape as *Diplodocus*, but much smaller – only about as tall as an adult human. Another difference was that it spent more time walking on two legs than on four.

Megalosaurus

Lived: Middle Jurassic

Size: 9 metres long

Diet: Meat

Remains of a *Megalosaurus* were found in England in 1822, making it the first dinosaur described by scientists. It was closely related to *Allosaurus* and other theropod predators, running on two legs to catch prey before biting off chunks of meat with its serrated teeth.

Megatherium

Lived: Early Pliocene to Late Pleistocene

Size: 6 metres long

Diet: Plants

Like its relative *Glossotherium*, this large animal was a ground sloth, but it was about the size of an elephant. The massive size of this slow animal was enough to prevent predators from attacking. It could stand on its hind legs to reach up into trees to feed.

M

MAMMALS

You are a mammal, part of the same family that includes cats, dogs, elephants and dolphins. Mammals are warm-blooded and covered with fur. Nearly all mammals give birth to live young, which feed on milk. It was about 200 million years ago that the earliest mammals lived. Mammals and reptiles share a **common ancestor**. But over millions of years, these two groups evolved in different directions, and they now look completely different.

Side by Side

Early mammals lived during the time when dinosaurs ruled the land. The first mammals were about the size of modern-day mice and these tiny creatures fed on plants or hunted at night, when most dinosaurs were less active. They often lived in trees or in underground burrows to stay safe.

After the Dinosaurs

Many mammal species were able to survive the events that killed most of the last dinosaurs. They had fur to keep warm and their small size meant they could survive with very little food. Without dinosaurs as predators, mammals were now able to evolve and grow. Some prehistoric species, such as *Megatherium* and *Mammuthus*, were huge. They were about the size of modern Asian elephants. Many of these large mammals became extinct by the end of the Pleistocene, about 11,000 years ago. Human hunting may have been one of the causes.

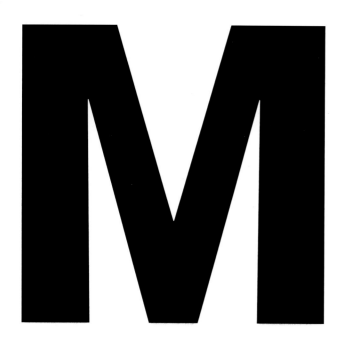

M

MODERN DINOSAURS

There are probably dinosaurs living in your town –
maybe even in your garden! Most scientists now
agree that birds are a form of dinosaur, making
them the only dinosaurs still living today. Birds are
now classified as theropods, the group of dinosaurs
that included *Tyrannosaurus rex*.

Bird or Dinosaur?

It is easy to look at some bird species, such as the
ostrich, and see similarities to the two-legged
hunters in the theropod group. An ostrich has
powerful hind limbs for running, and its feet are
covered with scales. Like dinosaurs, birds lay
eggs. Beneath the skin, a bird's skeleton has
many similarities to a dinosaur's skeleton.
One of these is the wishbone, formed by two
collarbones fused together. Many theropod
dinosaurs also had a wishbone.

Common Ancestor

Don't be fooled into thinking that the mighty *Tyrannosaurus rex* evolved into a little hummingbird. Many of the early theropods were fairly small, and the species that eventually evolved into birds branched off from the family tree long before *Tyrannosaurus rex* appeared. So there is not a straight line leading from *Tyrannosaurus rex* to the hummingbird – instead, they share a common ancestor thousands of generations back.

Notharctus

Lived: Eocene

Size: Up to 45 centimetres long

Diet: Plants (and possibly insects too)

This small mammal looked a lot like today's lemurs. It had a flexible body with long arms and legs and hands built for grasping. It lived in dense tropical forests, where it would have easily been able to climb through the trees as it looked for food.

Nothosaurus

Lived: Middle to Late Triassic

Size: 4 metres long

Diet: Meat

Nothosaurus was at home in the water as well as on land. It looked a bit like an *Ichthyosaurus*, but its limbs were more like legs than flippers, with webbed feet to help it to move through the water. *Nothosaurus* likely lived on land but went into the water to hunt. Its long, thin teeth were useful for trapping slippery fish.

Ophthalmosaurus

Lived: Middle to Late Jurassic

Size: Up to 6 metres long

Diet: Meat

Ophthalmosaurus was related to *Ichthyosaurus*, but it had very large eyes, which give it its name. These eyes may have allowed it to see and hunt prey in deep water. Although it was a reptile, palaeontologists have found remains of several pregnant females. This shows that *Ophthalmosaurus* gave birth to live young.

Ouranosaurus

Lived: Early Cretaceous

Size: 7 metres long

Diet: Plants

The sail or fin running along the spine of an *Ouranosaurus* resembled that of *Spinosaurus*, which also lived during the Cretaceous period. But *Spinosaurus* was a fierce predator, while *Ouranosaurus* was a herbivore that probably grazed on reeds and other low-growing plants along riverbanks.

Oviraptor

Lived: Late Cretaceous

Size: 2 metres long

Diet: Plants and meat

Palaeontologists originally gave this dinosaur a name meaning 'egg thief'. However, they later discovered that the fossils they found were probably guarding their own nest rather than raiding those of other dinosaurs. These small dinosaurs had no teeth, but their curved jaws would have been capable of crushing eggshells or shellfish. Their bodies may have had a covering of feathers.

P

Pachycephalosaurus

Lived: Late Cretaceous

Size: 8 metres long

Diet: Plants

The thick, bony dome on this dinosaur's head was surrounded by hard knobs and sharp spikes. These domes were originally thought to be used for head-butting, but now some palaeontologists think they may have been for attracting mates or recognizing each other.

Pakicetus

Lived: Eocene

Size: Up to 1.8 metres long

Diet: Meat

Pakicetus is one of the earliest ancestors of today's whales, though it didn't look much like a whale. It was the size of a large dog and had legs capable of walking on land. The shape of its ears makes palaeontologists think that it spent more time on land than in water. However, it probably dived into water to catch fish to eat.

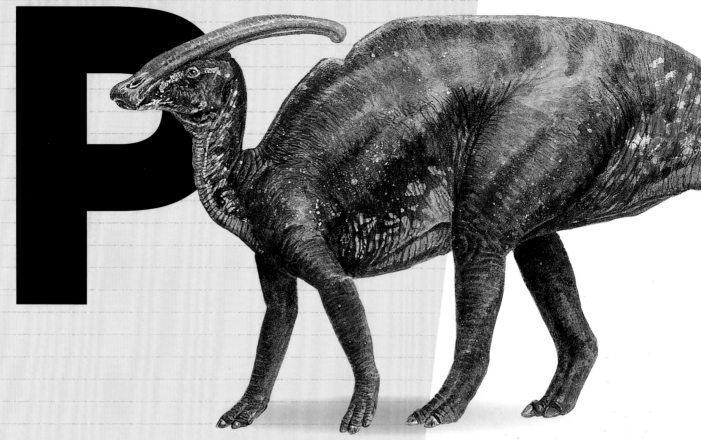

P

Parasaurolophus

Lived: Late Cretaceous

Size: 11 metres long

Diet: Plants

This duck-billed dinosaur had an impressive hollow crest on its head, which could be up to 1.5 metres long. Some palaeontologists think that the hollow crest may have allowed this duck-billed dinosaur to make loud trumpeting sounds.

Procoptodon

Lived: Pleistocene

Size: 2 metres tall

Diet: Plants

Remains of *Procoptodon*, which was similar in size and shape to a kangaroo, have been found in Australia. It would have grazed on plants, using its height to reach branches that smaller animals could not. *Procoptodon* could move quickly to escape predators, and it may also have used its large feet to kick out in defence.

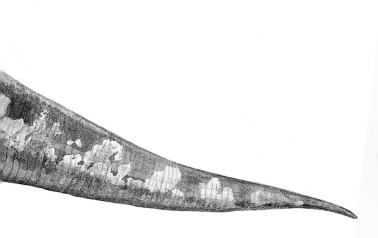

Peltobatrachus

Lived: Late Permian

Size: 60 centimetres long

Diet: Meat and insects

This early amphibian has a name meaning 'shield frog', and it had bony armour plates covering its body, a little like an armadillo. Palaeontologists think that this slow-moving creature lived mainly on land but returned to the water to lay its eggs, much like modern frogs.

P

Pteranodon

Lived: Late Cretaceous

Size: Wingspan of 5.5 metres or more

Diet: Fish

Many people think that *Pteranodon* was a dinosaur, but although it lived at the same time, it was a pterosaur (flying reptile) rather than a dinosaur. Its long, toothless jaws were similar to those of a pelican. The crest on its head was larger in males than in females. Although the crest may have helped *Pteranodon* to steer as it flew, some palaeontologists think it is more likely that it helped individuals to recognize each other.

P

PALAEONTOLOGY

Palaeontologists are often known as 'dinosaur hunters', but their job is much more than that. They study the remains of all prehistoric plants and animals, not just dinosaurs.

Geology

A palaeontologist needs to understand geology – the study of the Earth and its rocks. Fossils are usually found in rock, and the position of a fossil can give clues about when it was formed. Palaeontologists also use other methods, such as analyzing a fossil's chemical make-up.

Palaeontology or Archaeology?

People sometimes get confused about the difference between palaeontologists and **archaeologists** – after all, they both dig into the ground to find clues about the past. But archaeologists are focused on human remains and the objects that humans left behind. Palaeontologists study the fossils of ancient plants and animals.

Putting It All Together

Finding a fossil is only the first part of the job. A palaeontologist must analyze each fossil to discover what kind of animal or plant it belonged to. They look into how their finding may relate to other fossils. They are often able to figure out what an animal would have looked like from just a handful of bones.

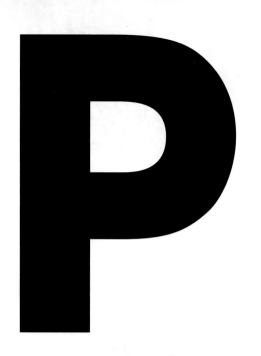

PREDATORS AND PREY

Some carnivores may have scavenged meat from bodies that were already dead, but many of them hunted live animals. They used speed and strength, combined with sharp teeth and claws, to catch their prey.

How Do We Know?

Palaeontologists have found evidence that shows what different species ate. If the contents of a dinosaur's stomach were fossilized along with the rest of its body, that can show what its last meal was. Fossilized dinosaur poo can also show what they ate. There have also been discoveries of tooth marks on bones, and sometimes even a whole tooth lodged in the bone!

Working Together

Some species of carnivores, such as *Velociraptor*, may have hunted in packs, as wolves do. However, it is very difficult to figure out an animal's behaviour from its fossil. There have been finds where several predator fossils of the same species were clustered around a single prey. This could mean that the predators were hunting together when a flood or landslide killed them all. But it could also mean that the predators were scavenging, or that they were fighting over a carcass that one of them had killed.

Q

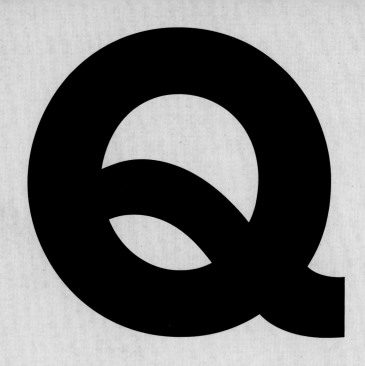

Quetzalcoatlus

Lived: Late Cretaceous

Size: Wingspan of up to 11 metres

Diet: Meat

Nearly as tall as a giraffe and with huge wings for soaring through the sky, *Quetzalcoatlus* was one of the largest flying reptiles. On the ground, it used its wings as front limbs so that it could walk on all fours. Palaeontologists think that *Quetzalcoatlus* used its sharp, pointed beak to catch lizards and small mammals. If it hunted near the banks of a river it would have been able to grab fish and amphibians.

R

Rhomaleosaurus

Lived: Early Jurassic

Size: Up to 7 metres long

Diet: Meat

Rhomaleosaurus was a large, long-necked pliosaur that swam through the oceans during the Early Jurassic. All of the known remains of this creature have been found in England. Despite its size, the shape of its teeth makes palaeontologists think that it probably ate small fish and squid. It may have been able to smell blood in the water to help it to find prey.

Robertia

Lived: Middle to Late Permian

Size: 15 centimetres long

Diet: Plants

This early burrowing creature was a therapsid – a member of
a group that includes mammals and their ancestors. It looked
a bit like a naked mole rat, with two downward-pointing tusks
in its upper jaws. It probably used its claws to dig for roots and
to carve out burrows for hiding from predators.

Sauropelta

Lived: Early Cretaceous

Size: 7 metres long

Diet: Plants

Sauropelta belonged to a group that were the ancestors of *Ankylosaurus* and other armoured dinosaurs. Their armour was not as thick and heavy, but they were still very slow-moving. *Sauropelta* had large spikes on its neck that would have given it some protection against predators.

Smilodon

Lived: Pleistocene

Size: Up to 1 metre tall at the shoulder

Diet: Meat

Smilodon is better known as the sabre-toothed tiger. It was about the size of a modern lion, and its 20-centimetre-long teeth made it a fearsome predator. Palaeontologists believe that it sometimes hunted early humans. It may have dropped down onto its prey from rocks or tree branches. *Smilodon* also would have attacked much larger animals such as the mastodon.

S

Spinosaurus

Lived: Late Cretaceous

Size: Up to 18 metres long

Diet: Meat

Spinosaurus was a huge theropod – taller and longer than *Tyrannosaurus rex* and *Giganotosaurus*, but not as heavy. It looked even bigger thanks to the massive sail along its back, supported by spines up to 1.8 metres long. *Spinosaurus* ate fish, and it probably waded into the water to reach down and catch them in its crocodile-like jaws. It may even have been able to swim.

S

Stegosaurus

Lived: Late Jurassic

Size: 9 metres long

Diet: Plants

Stegosaurus is well known for the bony plates that stood up from its back. However, no one is quite sure what they were for! They are not likely to have been for protection against predators – the spikes on its tail were *Stegosaurus's* main line of defence. However, they may have made predators less likely to attack by making *Stegosaurus* look bigger. The plates may have helped the dinosaur to regulate its body temperature, or maybe helped members of the species to recognize each other.

S SKELETONS

When an animal dies, the skin, muscles and organs are either eaten or rot away. If the animal ends up turning into a fossil, usually only the hardest parts, such as the bones and teeth, are preserved. This is why the dinosaurs that you see in museums are usually just skeletons.

In the Ground

When a palaeontologist finds a fossil, sometimes the bones are all there, in the positions they would have been when the animal was alive. But very few finds are like that! In other fossils, the bones are all jumbled up, and it's very common for some of them to be missing. Sometimes a single bone is found on its own.

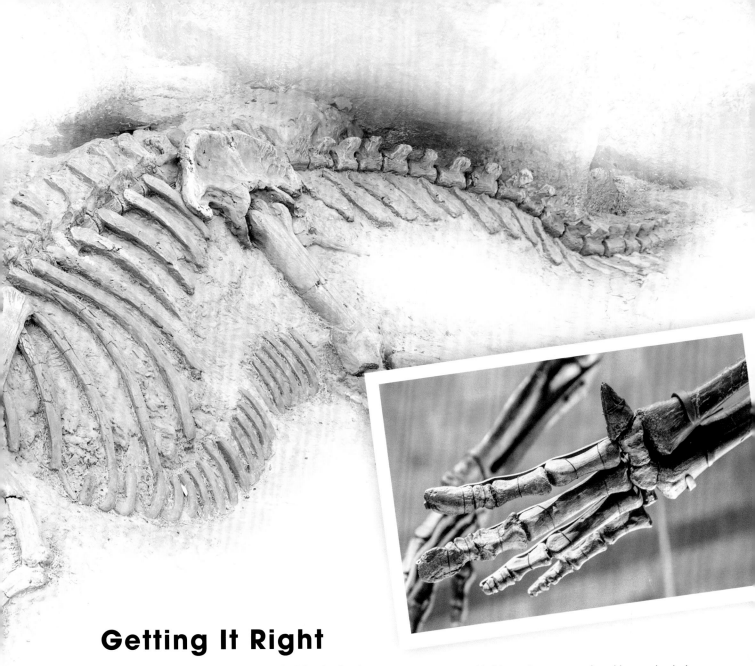

Getting It Right

It's a palaeontologist's job to arrange all the bones in the right positions and to work out how to fill in any gaps. Sometimes they don't get it quite right. For example, an early find of an *Iguanodon* fossil included a bony spike. Some modern iguanas had a horn on their face, so that's where the palaeontologist assumed that the *Iguanodon* spike went. It was decades later before another fossil discovery showed that the spike actually belonged on the dinosaur's hand.

SWIMMING REPTILES

Dinosaurs may have ruled the land, but there were many reptiles during prehistoric times that were adapted to live in water. They shared the oceans with fish and shellfish such as **ammonites**.

Ichthyosaurs

Various species of ichthyosaurs lived during the time of the dinosaurs. They looked a bit like whales or dolphins. Like those animals, they gave birth to live young and had to come to the surface to breathe. Ichthyosaurs could swim quickly to catch fish and other prey.

Powerful Predators

Towards the end of the Triassic, plesiosaurs first appeared, with their relatives the pliosaurs not far behind. Both groups used four flippers to swim, but plesiosaurs had small heads and long necks, while pliosaurs had larger heads and shorter necks. Plesiosaurs ate fish, while fierce pliosaurs often hunted larger prey, such as ichthyosaurs.

Land or Sea?

How is it possible that palaeontologists have found so many fossils of swimming reptiles on land? It's all due to the fact that the Earth has changed since the age of the dinosaurs. Back then, the climate was warmer and large parts of the planet were under water, including many regions that are now dry land.

T

Triceratops

Lived: Late Cretaceous

Size: Up to 9 metres long

Diet: Plants

With its three long horns and huge neck frill, *Triceratops* is instantly recognizable. This slow-moving herbivore lived at the same time as *Tyrannosaurus rex*, which often hunted it. *Triceratops* would have used its horns in self-defence, and there is evidence that the males sometimes used them against each other in battle.

T

Trilobite

Lived: Cambrian to Permian

Size: Up to 30 centimetres long

Diet: Meat

These small, ancient creatures were **arthropods**, a group linked by their jointed **exoskeletons**. The lobsters and insects that live today are arthropods, but *Trilobites* first appeared about half a billion years ago! Most of them were tiny, and they all had bodies divided into three sections. They lived in the oceans and ate worms or filtered food from the mud on the ocean floor.

Tsintaosaurus

Lived: Late Cretaceous

Size: 11.9 metres long

Diet: Plants

Tsintaosaurus was a large duck-billed dinosaur. Early fossil finds made palaeontologists think that it had a long, thin, forward-pointing crest on its head, making it look like the unicorn of dinosaurs. However, more recent research shows that these bones probably formed a hollow, domed crest more like that found on *Lambeosaurus*.

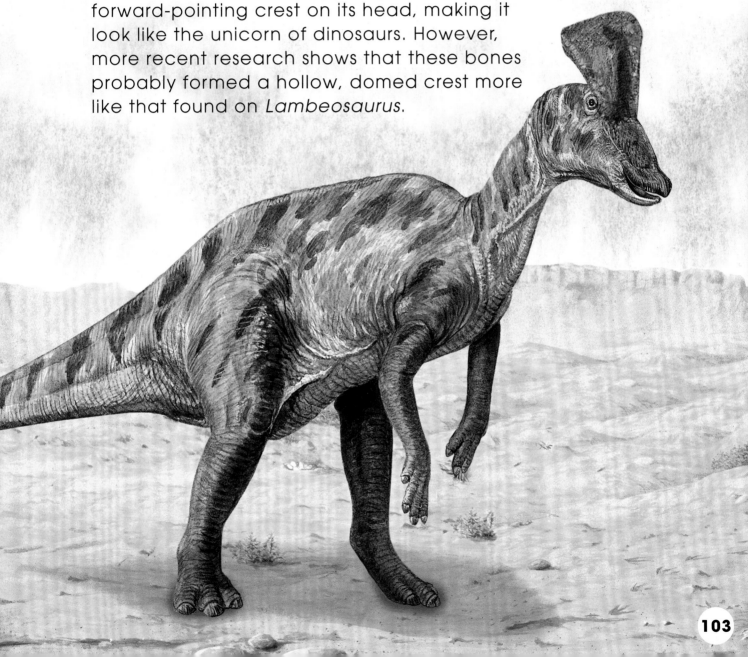

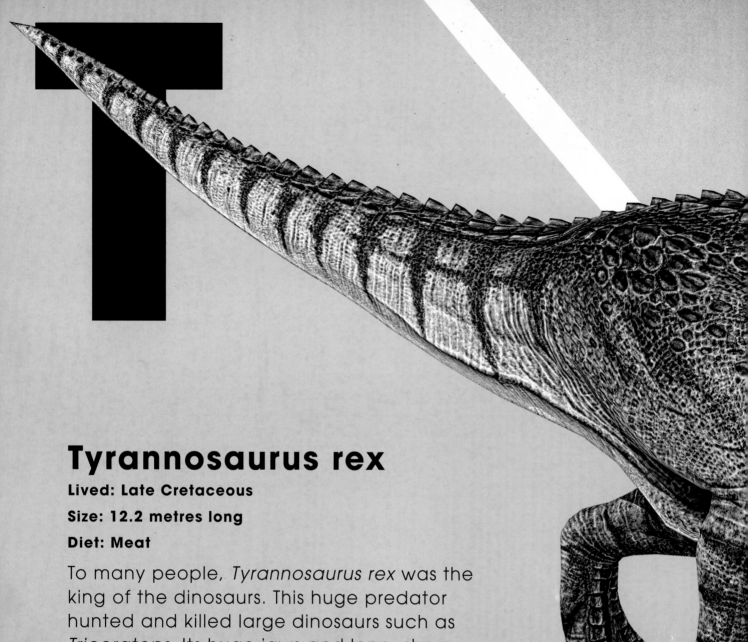

Tyrannosaurus rex

Lived: Late Cretaceous

Size: 12.2 metres long

Diet: Meat

To many people, *Tyrannosaurus rex* was the king of the dinosaurs. This huge predator hunted and killed large dinosaurs such as *Triceratops*. Its huge jaws and long, sharp, serrated teeth were perfect for tearing chunks of flesh from its victims. It could even crunch through bone! *Tyrannosaurus rex* became extinct, along with many other species, when an asteroid crashed into the Earth about 66 million years ago, causing huge changes to the Earth's climate.

U

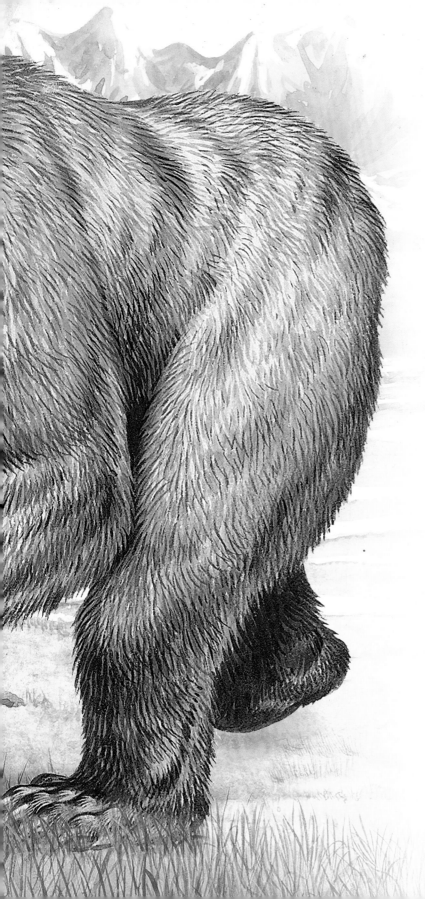

Ursus Spelaeus

Lived: Pleistocene

Size: Up to 3 metres long

Diet: Meat and plants

Better known as the cave bear, this large mammal existed at the same time as early humans. It seems to have lived in caves, possibly in groups. It mainly ate plants, but palaeontologists think that it sometimes ate meat as well – either by catching prey or by scavenging dead bodies. Early humans hunted cave bears, and some groups may have worshipped them too.

Velociraptor

Lived: Late Cretaceous

Size: Up to 1.8 metres long

Diet: Meat

It's easy to see why this dinosaur was given a name that means 'speedy thief'. It was small but fast-moving, running on its two hind legs. Its feet each had a large, sharp claw on one toe. Palaeontologists now think that this dinosaur's body was covered with feathers. The feathers would have provided insulation to help to keep it warm.

Vieraella

Lived: Early Jurassic

Size: 2.5 centimetres long

Diet: Unknown

This tiny creature is the earliest frog ever found, living more than 200 million years ago. It looked remarkably similar to today's frogs, with back legs that were adapted for leaping. Palaeontologists have only found one fossil of this species – an impression of it left in rock. As a result, there is still a lot that we don't know about this ancient little frog.

Wiwaxia

Lived: Early to Middle Cambrian

Size: Up to 5 centimetres long

Diet: Microorganisms

This odd little creature lived in the very early days of complex life on Earth. It had a small, soft, oval-shaped body that inched along a bit like a slug. But *Wiwaxia's* body was covered with scales and spines that would have protected it from predators. Its mouth was on the underside of its body and was used to scrape tiny living things off the sea floor.

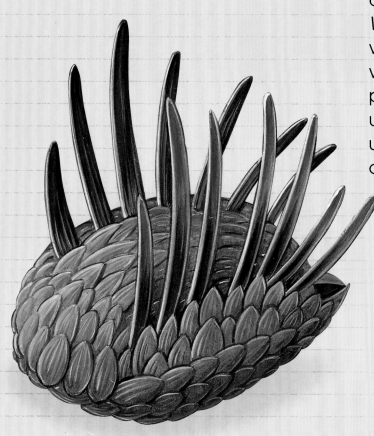

X

Xenacanthus

Lived: Devonian to Late Triassic

Size: Up to 90 centimetres long

Diet: Meat

This ancestor of modern sharks survived on Earth for a very long time – about 150 million years. Its small body was shaped more like an eel than the sharks we know today. It lived and hunted in freshwater rather than the oceans. *Xenacanthus* had a long, sharp spine at the back of its head that may have protected it from predators.

Y

Yangchuanosaurus

Lived: Late Jurassic

Size: Up to 10.7 metres long

Diet: Meat

This large theropod looked similar to its relative, *Allosaurus*. However, *Yangchuanosaurus* had an unusually long tail – about half the total length of its body. Its remains have been found in Asia, where it would have hunted stegosaurs and sauropods. It was first discovered in 1977 by a construction worker building a dam.

Yochelcionella

Lived: Early Cambrian

Size: Less than 2.5 centimetres

Diet: Unknown

This tiny mollusc had a cone-shaped shell that made it look like a snail. It lived in the water, and its shell had a straw-shaped snorkel that helped it to breathe by allowing wastewater to flow away from its gills. Palaeontologists have found many examples of their shells in the fossil record, and have divided *Yochelcionella* into several different species.

Z

Zalambdalestes

Lived: Late Cretaceous

Size: Up to 20 centimetres long

Diet: Insects

Zalambdalestes was a mammal that looked similar to a mouse. It had a long snout and tail, and it may have moved around by hopping like a rabbit. It would have hunted for insects in the forest undergrowth, using its sharp teeth to grab whatever it could catch. *Zalambdalestes* would have made a tasty meal for small, carnivorous dinosaurs.

Zygorhiza

Lived: Late Eocene

Size: About 6 metres long

Diet: Meat

Zygorhiza was a type of early whale, with a toothed jaw that helped it to catch fish and mammals that lived in the ocean. Its skeleton shows that unlike modern whales, it could flex its elbow. This has led some palaeontologists to think that it may have been able to come onto land to give birth, like modern seals. However, its large size would have made moving around on land difficult.

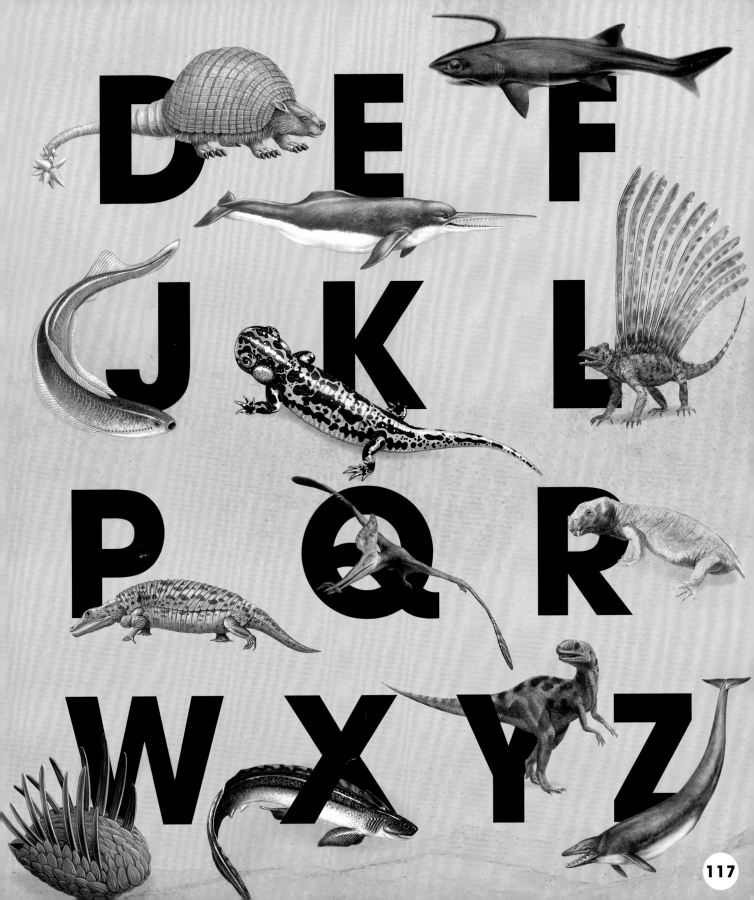

GLOSSARY

Ammonites: a group of extinct cephalopods from the Mesozoic era that had flat, spiral shells divided into chambers

Amphibian: an animal that lives in water for part of its life, often when it is young, and on land for another part

Ancestors: past species that changed very slowly over generations to become a more recent or existing species or group

Archaeologists: scientists who study the material remains of past human life, such as tools, pottery, jewellery and monuments

Arthropods: creatures that are cold-blooded and have segmented bodies, many jointed limbs, and have an external skeleton, such as crabs, spiders, centipedes and butterflies

Asteroid: a small, rocky object that orbits the Sun

Atmosphere: all of the air surrounding the Earth

Burrows: holes or tunnels dug in the ground by an animal for shelter

Carnivores: animals that mainly eat meat

Cartilage: a bendable, flexible tissue that connects bone together, and can also be found in the ear and nose

Climate: the weather conditions in a particular place over a long period of time

Common ancestor: an ancestor that two or more descendants have in common

Continents: very large areas of land. The Earth currently has seven continents, but over millions of years, continents can join together or split apart

Crest: a structure on the top of the head of several dinosaur species

Duck-billed: having flattened jaws that are similar to the bill of a modern duck

Evolved: changed over many generations in order to become better adapted to the local environment

Exoskeletons: supportive or protective shell-like skins covering the outside of the body

Extinct: having died out completely as a species, so that no more are left

Fossils: the remains or impressions of a prehistoric plant or animal that have been preserved in rock

Frill: a curving bony plate that extended behind the skull of some species of dinosaurs, such as *Triceratops*

Geologists: scientists who study the Earth and its processes

Habitats: places where plants or animals naturally live

Herbivores: animals that mainly eat plants

Herds: groups of animals

Mammals: animals that are warm-blooded, have hair or fur, and nearly always give birth to live young, which they feed with milk

Palaeontologists: scientists who study the remains of prehistoric plants and animals

Predators: animals that hunt other animals for food

Prey: animals that are hunted by other animals for food

Pterosaurs: members of a family of flying reptiles that lived at the same time as the dinosaurs

Reptiles: members of a group of animals, including snakes, lizards and turtles, that have dry scaly skin and mostly lay eggs on land

Sauropod: a type of large dinosaur that walked on four legs, ate plants and had a long neck and tail

Scavenging: finding dead bodies in order to eat their meat, instead of hunting animals for food

Serrated: having a jagged edge, like a saw

Species: a group of plants or animals that all have the same features and can produce young together

Theropods: carnivorous dinosaurs that walked on two legs

Vertebrates: animals with a backbone or spine

Picture Credits

t = top, b = bottom, l = left, r = right, c = centre